STO

FRIENDS
OF ACPL

D1541765

A FIRST BIOGRAPHY

ELI WHITNEY
and the
MACHINE AGE

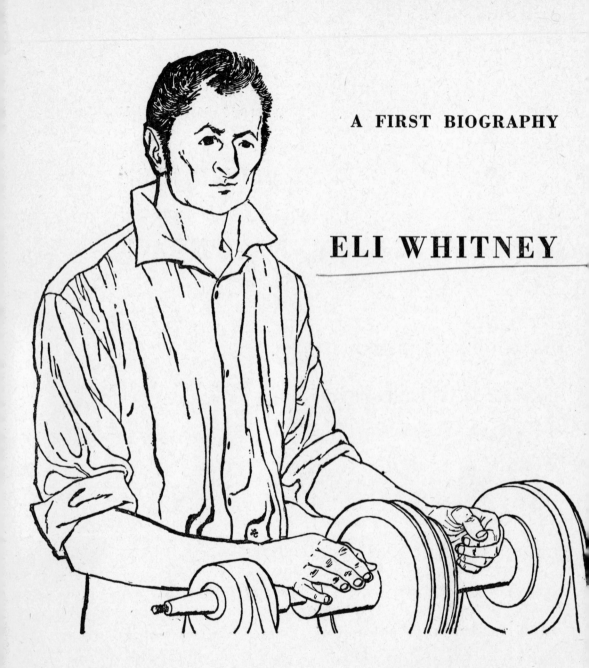

A FIRST BIOGRAPHY

ELI WHITNEY

and the MACHINE AGE

by WILMA PITCHFORD HAYS

pictures by ALFRED PETERSEN

jB.
W612h

FRANKLIN WATTS, INCORPORATED

575 Lexington Avenue   New York 22, N. Y.

THE AUTHOR is grateful for permission to use information and quotations from the following sources:

Eli Whitney Papers at the Yale University Library;

The World of Eli Whitney, by Jeannette Mirsky and Allan Nevins (New York: The Macmillan Company, 1952).

Library of Congress Catalog Card Number: 59-10957

© COPYRIGHT 1959 BY FRANKLIN WATTS, INC.
Manufactured in the United States of America

FIRST PRINTING

Contents

U. S. 1089393

Eli the Boy

On December 8, 1765, Eli and Elizabeth (Fay) Whitney looked at their first-born son. The baby had black hair. He was longer than most babies, even his nose was long, and he cried hard for what he wanted. They smiled and said that their boy seemed strong. He would grow up to be a big help to his father on the farm. They named him Eli after his father.

Eli Whitney was born in a young America, eleven years before the Thirteen Colonies declared themselves independent of England. Compared to England, America was a big land with almost unlimited raw materials, lumber, furs, and rich soil. Many men were needed to develop the new country, many more than were living in America. There was a shortage of skilled labor.

A man worked from sunup to sundown, but there was a limit to the amount of work he could do with his two hands and the few tools available. The few roads in the new land were little more than paths. Travel was difficult and expensive. Even if a farmer undertook a journey to a city, there were not many household goods to buy.

Farmers depended upon themselves for almost everything they needed. Each farmer had his own workshop near his house or barn. Here he built chairs and tables and other things necessary for his farm and home.

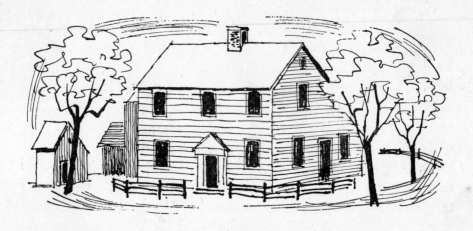

Eli Whitney's father had such a workshop on his farm in West-borough, Massachusetts. At an early age, Eli was spending much of his time in the shop. Young Eli loved to tinker and whittle and fix anything he could find that needed repair. When he was eight, he took apart his father's watch and put it back together again in perfect running order. Later, he saw a violin and made one in his father's shop, which surprised everyone by playing good music. His father soon saw that Eli's younger brothers, Josiah and Ben, were more help on the farm than Eli.

Eli's sister Elizabeth, who loved her oldest brother dearly, wrote in letters to friends, "Our Father had a work shop and sometimes made wheels of different descriptions. He had a lathe to turn chairposts and quite a variety of tools. This gave my Brother an opportunity of learning the use of tools very young. He lost no time, as soon as he could handle tools he was always making something in the shop and seemed not to relish working on the farm."

Some time after his mother's death, Eli's father married again. Eli's stepmother had a set of fine knives which had been made in England. She was very proud of the knives. Eli told her that he could make just such a knife if he had the tools, and he could *make the tools to make the knife* if he had the proper materials. His stepmother thought he was bragging. But shortly after one of her knives broke, she changed her mind. Eli brought her a knife which he had made, and it was almost as fine as her other knives. Even more astonishing, Eli had made the tools to make the knife, just as he said he could.

Eli the Young Business Man

When the Revolutionary War began, young America found itself in need of many things which it had always bought from England—cloth, tools, nails, and muskets. America managed to buy muskets from France, but nails were almost impossible to get and brought a high price. Eli asked his father to put a forge in their shop so Eli could make nails to sell.

Eli not only made nails but he fashioned tools by hand so he could work faster and make better nails. His business grew and he began to make tools to sell to other people. One day he rode his father's horse to visit shops about the countryside. When he returned, he had hired a man to work for him.

Eli had learned many things watching others work in the shops he visited. He told his sister Elizabeth that he should be able to

make a profit from the work of the man he had hired, since it would take no more coal for two men to work at the forge than one. Eli was about fifteen when he undertook this business of his own.

After the end of the Revolutionary War, English nails were sold again more cheaply in America than Eli could make them. He began to think of something else he could make that people would buy. He saw that women had quit tying on their bonnets. It was the fashion now to fasten hats with long hatpins. Eli began making hatpins as well as he had made nails. Later he made walking canes for men.

When Eli Whitney was about nineteen, he told his family that he planned to go to college. He was almost a man now, six feet tall. Wouldn't he feel strange among the younger college boys? they asked. It was true that the hatpin and walking-cane business was no longer profitable, but Eli was known for the skill in his hands. He could always make a living without more education.

Few young men went to college, and those who did go planned to enter some profession, such as law or teaching or the ministry.

Eli said that perhaps he would study law. The neighbors told Eli's father that college would ruin one of the best mechanics in the country.

Eli seemed to want knowledge in his head to equal the skill in his hands. He declared that he was going to college somehow. His father told him that he could help with a few college expenses, but a farmer had very little cash. Eli would have to earn most of his own way.

Hearing that the neighboring town of Grafton needed a schoolmaster, Eli borrowed his father's horse and rode there. He came home to tell his family that he had been accepted as a teacher. His father was astonished to think that his son believed he could teach when Eli had to go to school himself to learn enough to enter college.

Eli managed to do both—to teach and to go to school. When he wasn't teaching, he was studying. His teaching days were long,

spent in a one-room schoolhouse. Eli had to start a fire in the fire-place almost every morning before class. His pupils sat in a row on benches before a desk that was only a wooden shelf nailed to the wall.

Here Eli taught the children to copy numbers on coarse brown paper. He taught them to write carefully with a quill pen and ink.

Some of the boys and girls found it hard to make the coils and curves that all good penmen drew in writing letters of the alphabet then. Eli saw that his pupils could do their best work only when they had a good pen. He made a large sample of a quill pen as a model for his pupils to make their own.

Eli and College

Eli Whitney was twenty-three years old when, finally, he was ready to go to Yale College in New Haven, Connecticut for his entrance examinations. He satisfied Yale's President Stiles that he had learned Latin and Greek, the classics, English grammar, and arithmetic.

During his college years, Eli woke each morning about five. In winter his room was cold. He dressed as fast as he could, washed at an outside pump, and went off to chapel for an hour. A class followed chapel, then breakfast. After this, there was study until noon. Lunch was followed by a free hour and then more study for a class at four. Then evening prayers, supper, and more study for the next morning's class. Eli also found time for odd jobs to make the extra money he needed to continue at Yale.

Yale College was small then, having about 125 students. President Stiles did a great deal of the lecturing himself. One of the best-educated men in America, he was interested in all that went on in the world, particularly the new knowledge in science. He saw to it that Yale's "museum," a kind of laboratory, was equipped with many of the instruments known at that time. Here, Eli learned the use of equipment from all over the world.

President Stiles sent to England for a small telescope, a micrometer, and an orrery. One of the instruments was broken when

it arrived. President Stiles was most disappointed. He told the class that it was such a delicate instrument he would have to return it to England for repair. No mechanic in America had the skill to repair it.

Eli Whitney said he believed he could repair it. At first, President Stiles was afraid to let him touch it. As Eli examined the instrument and seemed to understand its workings, President Stiles told him to go ahead.

Eli astonished President Stiles and the other students by putting the complicated instrument into good working order. He won their respect for the ability in his hands as well as for being a good student.

In his classes and in the library, Eli learned the new things which other men had done, and were doing, throughout the world. He learned the principle of Watt's steam engine. He learned that an ironmaster, John Wilkinson, had made the first metal cutting tool that did fairly accurate work. He heard of a machine designed by John Smeaton to manufacture cannon at an ironworks in England. Although Smeaton believed he had a good idea, he admitted that his machine didn't work very well. Smeaton said that "neither the tools nor workmen existed that could manufacture so complex a machine with sufficient precision."

As Eli Whitney learned of the work of other mechanics, designers, and industrialists, he must have wondered how their work could be improved upon and how their tools could be made to do better work. Such questions always set ideas working in Eli's head.

Eli wanted to learn all he could from classes but he wanted other things from college, too. He met young men from all parts of the

United States and made friends whom he would keep all his life. He learned how to dress and the manners that would help him feel at home with all kinds of people. He learned enough law to help him in business later. He learned how to express himself when speaking or writing; thus he was able to explain his ideas so that others could understand him.

There is little doubt that Eli Whitney's college education helped a talented mechanic to become a great inventor.

Eli Whitney and the Cotton Gin

Just before Eli Whitney's graduation from Yale College, he went home on vacation and told his family that he had been promised a teaching position in New York. He was happy to know that he had work and would be able to pay back the money he had borrowed for his last years in college.

When he returned to Yale for graduation, he found that a mistake had been made. He was not to have the New York job after all. President Stiles suggested that he see a Mr. Miller who was visiting in New Haven. Mr. Miller was looking for a tutor for the children of a planter in South Carolina. Eli needed money so badly

that he agreed to take the job, although he had not planned to go so far from home.

Thus Eli Whitney, the New England Yankee, went South. He traveled by boat with Mr. Miller and the woman for whom Miller worked, Mrs. Greene. She was the widow of the Revolutionary War hero, General Nathanael Greene. Mrs. Greene was a friendly woman. When they reached the South, she learned that Eli was again disappointed in his job. The tutoring position was to pay less than he had expected. She invited Eli to be a guest on her plantation while he decided what to do.

On Mrs. Greene's plantation, Eli Whitney saw cotton growing for the first time. Mrs. Greene held parties where Eli met neighboring planters. He heard them discussing how poor the South was and how much they needed a good paying crop to make their living.

Rice, corn, and potatoes were the main crops in the South then. Rice required so much labor to grow that it was not profitable. Corn and potatoes were grown mostly for local use as food. The planters needed a money crop, something they could export as well as sell locally.

Eli heard the planters say that England was begging for cotton since inventors in England had made machines which would weave cotton into cloth quickly. The South shipped its long-staple cotton to the manufacturers in England, but there wasn't enough long-staple cotton to keep the English manufacturers busy.

Eli asked why the planters didn't plant more long-staple cotton. They told him that long-staple cotton would grow only near the sea. It was often called "sea island cotton" or "lowland cotton." This lowland cotton had large black seeds which were easily removed by a simple machine with rollers. The seeds were rolled off and the long cotton fibers left clean.

Short-staple cotton, which would grow like a weed anywhere, even in the uplands, had clinging green seeds which could not be removed except by hand. One slave must work all day to pick the green seeds from one pound of short-staple cotton. Very little could be sold at this rate.

Ideas always began to buzz in Eli Whitney's head when there was need of tools to do some kind of work better. He wrote to his father, "There were a number of very respectable Gentlemen at Mrs. Greene's who all agreed that if a machine could be invented which would clean the cotton with expedition, it would be a great thing both to the Country and to the inventor."

A few days after he began thinking of a machine to clean cotton, the plan for an engine came to Eli. He told his idea to Mr. Miller, who managed the plantation for Mrs. Greene.

Miller was excited by the idea. He said he would raise the money to make the machines if Eli and he could be partners. Mrs. Greene thought Eli Whitney could make anything after he whittled an embroidery hoop for her better than any she could buy. She gave Eli the use of a shop on her plantation. Here he could work without other people knowing what he was doing. He knew that the South needed a cotton-cleaning machine so much that others would try to steal his idea if they could.

Some weeks later Eli completed the first model of his cotton gin (gin is short for engine). It worked so well that he wrote to one of his best friends in New Haven, a Mr. Stebbins, saying, "Dame fortune has turned about, and, for the first time, her Ladyship deigns to look upon me with a smiling face."

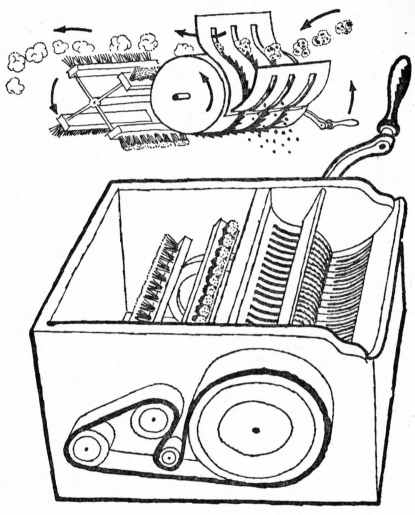

ELI WHITNEY'S COTTON GIN

Mrs. Greene invited some planter friends to her home to see Eli demonstrate his cotton gin. These men became excited when they saw that the machine really worked. Wire teeth pulled the cotton fibers through slatted holes small enough to leave the green seeds behind. A brush, on rollers, cleaned the cotton from the wire teeth.

At last the worthless green-seed cotton, which would grow abundantly anyplace, could be cleaned fast enough to be sold profitably. All the planters wanted a cotton gin.

Mr. Miller told them that he and Eli were partners. They planned to make a number of the gins and set them up in convenient shops throughout the South. Planters could bring their cotton to the shops and it would be ginned for a share in each cotton crop. The planters eagerly hurried home to tell the others about the gin.

The South was agricultural and did not have the materials or skilled labor to manufacture Eli's gins. Therefore Eli returned to New Haven, Connecticut to set up a shop where he could hire the mechanics he needed to make them.

When he applied for a patent for his cotton gin, he wrote to the Secretary of State, Thomas Jefferson, "That with the Ginn, if turned by horses or by water, two persons will clean as much cotton in one day, as a hundred persons could cleane in the same time with the ginns now in common use."

During the next year, Eli worked so hard getting his factory set up in New Haven that he could not find time even to visit his home. When he finally had gins ready to take to the South, he went to New York to borrow more money for his business. He fell ill with malaria and could not come home for several days. When he did return, he found that his shop had burned and, with it, all his gins, machines, and tools.

He wrote his father saying that he had toiled for more than two years, almost day and night, to make the tools and special machines needed to make his gins.

Now, all his labor seemed lost.

"I do not, however, despair," he wrote, "and hope I shall not sink under my misfortune."

Eli rebuilt his shop. Seven months later he had twenty-six cotton gins ready to ship South.

But luck was not with Eli Whitney. The cotton gin he had invented was being copied in the South by mechanics who had seen his gin demonstrated. Many of these copies were already at work on plantations and in shops.

Miller and Whitney went to court to protect their invention, but it was many years before the courts finally gave them a victory. Then Eli's patent ran out and his application for renewal was turned down.

The entire country profited greatly through Eli Whitney's idea and ability. One year after Eli had patented his gin, cotton exported from the United States rose from 138,328 pounds to 6,276,-000 pounds. Not long after, by 1800, the figure had risen to 17,790,-000 pounds exported, and cotton was called "King Cotton." It is easy to see how Eli's invention was of great importance to the economic growth of the United States in those early days.

The South particularly benefited. At last it had an export crop which supported the planters and helped raise the standard of living for all the people of the South.

Muskets for the Government

When Eli's cotton gin became public property, he was thirty-two years old, poor and overworked and heavily in debt. He was forced to discover another way of making a living.

He sat in his shop many nights alone trying to think what he could do. He must make something better than anyone else had made it before, something people needed. Any new idea or invention would require money. Eli already owed so much money to his friends and the bank that he could not ask for more. He tried to think of something the United States government needed. The government often advanced money on contracts for supplies.

Eli designed and made a screw press he hoped the government could use. He sent a drawing of the machine with instructions for using it to the government.

Secretary of the Treasury Wolcott wrote Eli that the government had already accepted a similar idea from another designer. However, Wolcott added that he was sorry and that he had been impressed by the "talents of Mr. Whitney."

Disappointed as he was, Eli was encouraged by Secretary Wolcott's letter. Eli asked himself what else the government might need that he could make better than it had been made before.

Now at this time, 1798, the young United States was faced with the possibility of war with its former friend, France, who was having trouble with England. France announced that she would hang sailors on American ships which carried cotton or other supplies to England and she would hang American seamen found working on English ships. French privateers sailed along the Atlantic coast and boarded, sometimes robbed, American ships almost within sight of home. The American people grew excited and angry over these abuses, and Congress appropriated thousands of dollars to buy muskets if war came.

Eli read in the newspapers of the money set aside for muskets and he knew there was no place America could buy them. France had supplied America with guns when the Colonies fought for their independence. But now all Europe seemed to be up in arms, and no country would sell muskets it might need for itself. Eli knew he had found something the government needed desperately.

Eli had never made a musket. He did not have a factory to make

23

muskets. He knew that gunsmiths were almost impossible to hire, there were so few of them. In fact there was a shortage of all skilled labor in America since everything made was fitted carefully by hand and each piece was individually different from every other.

Yet Eli Whitney did an astonishing thing. He wrote to the United States government and offered to make ten to fifteen thousand stand of arms if the government would sign a contract and advance him money to pay workmen and buy materials. A stand of arms was the musket, the bayonet, the ramrod, wiper, and screw driver.

There must have been a lot of headshaking when Secretary Wolcott first read Eli Whitney's proposal to other government officials. The government arsenal at Springfield had turned out only a thousand muskets in the past three years. The new arsenal at Harper's Ferry could do no better. Yet here was a private contractor who believed he could turn out ten thousand stand of arms and deliver them in a little more than two years.

The offer was unbelievable, but the United States needed muskets so badly that Eli was invited to Philadelphia to discuss a contract.

Even after Eli explained his idea to the few men gathered in Secretary Wolcott's office, they did not understand what he planned to do. Eli Whitney believed he could use machines to make parts for guns. Even more fantastic, Eli believed he could design and make machines which would work so perfectly that ordinary men, rather than trained gunsmiths, could be taught to run them. Eli even believed that his machines would make better parts for guns than skilled gunsmiths had been able to make by hand. He said he had tried out some of his ideas when making his cotton gins and he knew they would work.

The government officials were impressed by Eli Whitney's confidence in his own ability and ideas. They needed guns so desperately that they signed a contract with this man who didn't have a factory, raw materials, or machines to do what he promised to do. The government also signed many contracts with regular gunsmiths.

Eli Whitney returned to New Haven with $5,000 the government had advanced him and a model Charleville musket of 1763. This was the type musket which France supplied the United States during the Revolution. The government wanted it copied as closely as possible.

Eli began to work out his plans. He must design and make every machine himself *before* he could begin to make muskets. After his experience with the cotton gin, Eli made up his mind not to patent another invention. He kept his plans in his head. His idea was so revolutionary that he was not afraid of others stealing it, even if they saw him working on his machines.

Eli Whitney's Factory

Before Eli Whitney could make machines to make guns, he must have a shop in which to build them. He bought a millsite in the town of Hamden, which joined New Haven on the north.

In his first letter to Secretary Wolcott offering to make the muskets, Eli had mentioned this millsite. He said that there was a good fall of water here which could be used to run his machinery and, if he were awarded a contract, he would buy the millsite and build a gun factory at once. However, he could not buy or build until he had the contract and money from the government.

After he received his contract, Eli tried to do everything at once. He sent for workmen as far away as Massachusetts. He sent a ship to Philadelphia to bring back four thousand gunstocks from the government stores before the rivers would ice over. He wrote to dealers and manufacturers of iron to place orders for materials.

Eli worked fast but winter came early that year. The building of his factory was delayed by heavy snowstorms. The long bitter cold stopped men from working on the dam which was to run his machinery.

In the spring Eli Whitney was forced to write to Secretary Wolcott, "The season proved such that neither ore could be dug nor coals burned . . . & I have not received a single pound of iron from that quarter. The man with whom I contracted to weld my

Barrels failed—this would have been a great disappointment if I had met with no other."

In addition yellow fever broke out and many men were too ill to work. These handicaps delayed Eli's work so much that, when time came to deliver the first shipment of muskets, he had not a single gun to send. He wrote letters to Secretary Wolcott and gained more time. But eventually the government threatened to cancel Eli's contract and make him repay all the money he had been granted to start his factory.

Rumors had reached the government from visitors at Eli's shop. Whitney had promised ten to fifteen thousand stand of arms, yet there were no muskets in his buildings. True, there were *parts* of guns stacked in one shop, but none were put together. It would be years before the few gunsmiths Whitney could hire would be able to file and fit the guns he had promised.

Whitney had used government money to make a lot of new machines. But what had machines to do with making guns?

Worried officials met to discuss what was to be done. Anyone knew how long it took a skilled gunsmith to make a gun. A gunsmith might buy the barrel already welded, but he must bore it on a lathe. Then grind and file it carefully to make it true. Then carve a stock and fit it to the barrel. He must forge lock plates and file the lock parts, testing them over and over again with all the other parts until each fit. Then he must put all the parts together to see if they fit. When he was satisfied, he would have to take the gun apart. These parts had to be hardened before the gunsmith put them back together again, all by hand. And *one* gun was completed. How many years would it take Whitney's gunsmiths to go through this process ten thousand times?

A cabinet member reminded the other officials that Eli Whitney could not hire enough skilled gunsmiths to make these guns. The shortage of labor was great in the United States. Many men had left jobs to go West and claim land of their own.

But Secretary Wolcott argued that guns were needed desperately. When the contract had been given, Whitney had said that he had an entirely new system for making guns. If this were true, it would be bad business to stop Whitney's work before he had a chance to show what he could do. Eli was invited to come to Washington, the new capital in the wilderness to which the government had recently moved from Philadelphia. He was to meet with heads of the government and show why he had not fulfilled his contract.

Eli Whitney and Interchangeable Parts

In December, 1800, Eli Whitney went to Washington and took with him a wooden chest containing parts for muskets. He knew it would be impossible to explain how his new system worked. No official would believe it unless he himself saw the guns put together.

There must have been plenty of excitement and curiosity about the new system which the inventor from New Haven claimed was so superior to the old hand method of making muskets. The greatest men of the nation were gathered to see Whitney's demonstration. The second President of the United States, John Adams, was there; as well as Thomas Jefferson, who would soon replace him. Secretary Wolcott, members of the cabinet, and high-ranking officers from the army and navy came.

It is said that the faces of these men showed disappointment and anger when Eli Whitney opened the large wooden chest on the table before them and took out *parts of* muskets. They had expected to see finished muskets. Their disappointment turned to bewilderment when Eli asked some of them to pick different parts and lay them on the table. Then, before their eyes, Eli put the parts together to make a musket. He used only screws and a screw driver; there was no vise or filing or fitting.

So that they could see that this was not the special magic of his

30

fingers, Eli asked an army general to choose any parts he wished and assemble a musket. The general did so.

Excitement broke out among the men about the table. They had seen muskets put together in minutes—and better muskets than skilled gunsmiths could make in hours or even days. How was it possible?

Eli explained his new system of interchangeable parts, which was to have a tremendous influence on the industrial development of America in later years.

With his machines, Eli said, he could make thousands of musket parts, each part exactly like any other. He had designed each machine to make one kind of part so perfectly that this part would fit into any musket. Guns would no longer be different. Even repairs would be easy now, since a broken part could be replaced by another exactly like it.

Equally important, the skill for making the guns now lay in the machines. Eli had designed and built his machine tools so well that he could easily train men and boys to run them. Eli's machines would not only make uniform, interchangeable parts, but the parts could be made in spite of the shortage of skilled labor.

Among the astonished officials, only Jefferson saw clearly what Eli meant. Jefferson said that he had seen this idea earlier in France. An inventor named Leblanc had realized the possibility of interchanging parts and of making machines to cut out parts by pattern. But Leblanc had not carried his idea as far as Whitney had done.

Eli Whitney's demonstration of interchangeable parts was successful. He was asked to finish his contract to supply muskets for the government.

The government officials who granted Eli more time and money were interested chiefly in muskets for the defense of the country. Eli Whitney wanted to make good muskets, but he was more interested in the machines and tools which could guide ordinary men to do better work than skilled workers had done by the old hand method. He turned his attention now to perfecting his machines.

With machines taking the place of skilled men, and water power turning the machines, Eli hoped to speed his work faster and faster.

But Eli ran into trouble with some of his men. Many designers liked making guns the old way. They were proud of their handwork, slow as it was. They did not want to run a machine that turned out hundreds of parts for guns, over and over, each part so much like every other part that it could be used in any one of a thousand guns. Grumbling, many skilled men left his factory.

Eli taught ordinary men to run his machines. He never seemed to have time to sleep now. He was always trying to discover a way to improve his machines to make them do a better job faster.

He wrote to Secretary Wolcott explaining some of his experiments, "I find I can forge the Guards faster, more exactly in their true shape & so they will require less work in fitting up than they would be cast in Brass after a perfect Pattern by an experienced founder. This is also the case with respect to several of the smaller limbs of the lock and mounting."

He went on to say, "One of my primary objects is to form the tools so the tools themselves will fashion the work and give each part its proportion—which when once accomplished, will give expedition, uniformity, and exactness to the whole."

Eli studied and found a way to package the guns so they would not rust in storage. He packed them into tight pine boxes.

He was always writing letters to the government to ask for more time and money to carry out his improvements. He wrote far and wide for the best raw materials—iron and brass. He often designed patterns and sent them with his orders to show the dealers exactly what he wanted to do with the materials.

34

U. S. 1089393

Eli Whitney had his own ideas about how to keep the men he trained so they would not quit and go elsewhere to work. He tried to hire men who had property and families in New Haven and wanted to remain there. He built a village for his workers beside his factory, the first mill village. Here he built stone homes which he rented cheaply to his men and their families—the first such homes built for workmen by an employer in the United States. He provided a boarding house with a housekeeper for his unmarried boy apprentices.

At last, in 1809, Eli was able to deliver the final shipment on his government order for ten thousand stand of arms. His muskets proved so superior to previous muskets, even those made in the government armories at Springfield and Harper's Ferry, that the old ways of making muskets was practically finished. Eli Whitney was recognized as a master of musket making.

Jefferson, now President, wrote to a friend, "Mr. Whitney is at the head of a considerable gun manufactory in Connecticut, and furnishes the United States with muskets, undoubtedly the best they receive."

Ten and a half years had passed between the time Eli Whitney signed the contract for the muskets and the final shipment. If Eli had been interested only in muskets, he could have completed the order in less time. Letters which he wrote to friends show that Eli was more interested in a *new and better way of manufacturing* than he was in the object manufactured. Although Eli did not call it by name, he was busy establishing the first machine-tool industry.

He wrote to his friend Stebbins, "I meet with many delays which I did not expect but cannot avoid. I am many times impatient and unhappy that I progress so slowly—at other times I look around & see that I have done a great Deal and feel more satisfied with the progress which I have made. But my principal solace arises from the consideration that my machinery and modes of doing the work will certainly answer a better purpose than any heretofore devised."

More Trouble for Eli Whitney

By the time Eli Whitney had proved that his system of inter-changeable parts and machine-tooled manufacturing was superior to the slow hand methods, the United States was on the verge of the War of 1812 with England. Eli Whitney's shop was known as one of the best private-arms factories in America. He signed a new contract with the government. He had every reason to hope that his business troubles were over.

But officials changed in Washington. A captain named Irvine was appointed the new Commissary General of Purchases. Captain Irvine wanted the government to buy a musket which he and another man had designed. He began to find fault with the muskets Whitney had sent to the government. He tried to cancel Eli's contract and refused money advances.

Already overworked, Eli Whitney had to enter a long battle for his rights. He wrote letter after letter to government officials answering the charges brought by Irvine. He made trips to Washington and talked to officials. During the long feud, Eli was often ill but he continued to run his shop and supply arms while the war lasted.

Once he wrote to his friend, Stebbins, "I live constantly out at my place & tho I have at least forty People around me every day —I am yet a solitary *Old Bachelor*. I am incessantly occupied in my business and after laboring hard thro' the day I am obliged to leave ten times so much undone (which ought to have been done) as I have in the course of the day accomplished, and lie down under a load of cares already almost unsupportable & still accumulating. I flatter myself that I shall not sink under it. I shall persevere to the End."

When the war ended, Eli Whitney sent a letter direct to the man who was the President, James Madison. With his letter, he sent copies of Irvine's charges against him and his answers; Eli's law studies proved useful here. He asked that a government agency handle his contract rather than the Commissary of Purchases, Captain Irvine.

Congress began to investigate the many duties of the War Department and to decide which ones should be handled by each agency. Congress placed the Ordnance Department in charge of all arms, those provided by outside contractors as well as by government armories. Later, a friend of Eli's, Captain Lee, was appointed head of the armory at Springfield. Having won his battle, Eli Whitney turned his attention once again to his own shop. He improved his machines and shared his new ideas freely with Captain Lee.

One of his most important new ideas was a milling machine which he built before 1818. Eli did not patent or try to keep his machine secret. It was quickly put into use by others, including the government armories.

Eli's milling, or turning, machine was a guided tool, driven by water, which turned out barrels for muskets. It had a vise which held the work to be shaped upon a plate. The cutting tool, with "tooth-type" cutters, rotated on its own axis. It could turn out complicated parts, each measured exactly to fit into other uniform parts. The milling machine shaped the muzzle. It turned and slit the many screws which held many parts together to make the completed whole. Eli's milling machine could make musket barrels faster and cheaper than they had ever been made before.

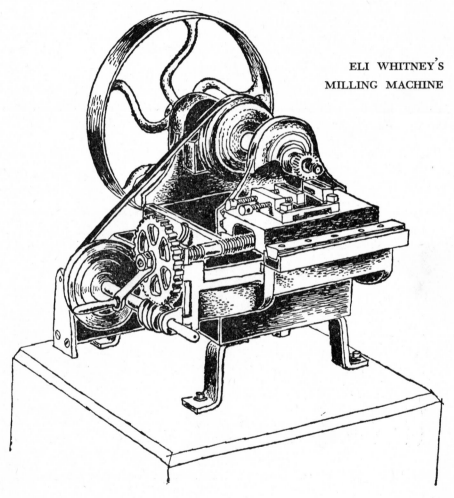

ELI WHITNEY'S
MILLING MACHINE

Eli Whitney and His Family

For twenty-three years the pressure of business and debts kept Eli Whitney from having much time for friends or family. His letters to them show that he was often lonely. He had taken his two nephews, Philos and Eli Whitney Blake, sons of his sister Elizabeth, into his shop when they were boys. They lived at his boarding house. Eli taught his nephews the business and sent Eli Whitney Blake to Yale.

WHITNEY DEMONSTRATES A DRILL PRESS TO HIS NEPHEWS

When Eli Whitney was fifty-one years old, he married Henrietta Edwards. She was thirty-one, daughter of his friend, the brilliant lawyer Pierpont Edwards. Eli was very happy when his own daughters, Frances and Elizabeth, were born; then a son, Eli Whitney, Jr.

His children were still very young when Eli became seriously ill. During the last years of his life, Eli not only ran his shop between illnesses, but invented things for friends and family to make their lives pleasanter.

He designed a better fireplace heater with cast-iron hearth to keep rooms warmer. Also a bureau for his wife in which all drawers locked by turning a key in the top drawer. (Today the same idea is used in office desks.)

He invented a cast-iron pump for Wolcott, a chemical apparatus for Professor Silliman at Yale. He even invented instruments needed for his own illness.

Eli Whitney was proud of the business he had built up under great difficulties. He planned his will so that his loved machines and shop would be kept in good hands until his son, Eli, Jr., was old enough to run the factory. Eli Whitney had trained his nephews to know the musket business. In his will, he provided that the two Blake boys would manage the factory at such a profit to themselves that they would surely remain at its head.

Eli Whitney, Jr., grew up and took over the factory. Whitney guns remained a family business for ninety years, when it was sold to Winchester Arms.

Other Uses of the
Interchangeable Parts Idea

Probably Eli Whitney never heard himself called "the father of mass production." While Eli lived, few people saw the great changes which his idea of interchangeable parts would make in industry.

From his idea was born mass production—that system of manufacturing which makes a standard dependable product swiftly and at the smallest cost. Because of its world leadership in mass production, American industry provides for Americans today one of the highest standards of living in the world.

Step by step, other men used Eli's ideas in other kinds of work. Many good mechanical designers throughout the world had been working alone on various ideas. Now they found that Eli Whitney's system of uniform, interchangeable parts suited their plans.

In Eli's time, clocks were made by hand from wood. Even the wheels, or works, inside the clock were carved from wood. Few families could own a clock, since a hand-made one was expensive.

A Connecticut clockmaker, Terry, used a handsaw to cut and a jacknife to whittle out his clocks. He sold each clock for about $40. An apprentice, Seth Thomas, worked for Terry. Later both these men set up rival mills and used machine-driven circular saws to make clocks. People thought they were crazy, but they made many more clocks by machine than by hand. They brought the price of clocks down to about $15.

Then clockmakers discovered that machines could cut parts for clocks from brass plates. Fine, eight-day brass clocks were made and sold at reasonable prices. Now that clocks were cheaper, more and more people wanted one so they would not have to depend upon the sun or an hourglass when they wished to measure time.

Suppose they had been told then that someday a family would own several clocks. Or that an alarm clock would ring to wake people in the morning. Or that a clock would turn on music by controlling dials on a small box called a radio. No one would have believed such fantastic claims, unless, perhaps, Eli Whitney.

Singer used Whitney's system of uniform, interchangeable parts to make sewing machines in quantity. Sewing machines could then be bought for use in the home, and women's work became easier. Once there were sewing machines, factories sprang up to make clothing. Women were hired to work outside their homes in these factories.

Shoes, which cobblers had made by hand to fit each person, came to be made in factories by machines. Then people could go into a store and buy shoes without waiting until the cobbler could find time to fill their orders.

Cyrus McCormick discovered ways to manufacture machinery needed on farms to plant and harvest food. His machines had a great influence on agriculture. With big fields of grain tended by machines, enough food could be grown on the farms to feed all those who worked in cities and towns.

CYRUS McCORMICK'S REAPER

Carriages drawn by horses were owned by the few people who could afford them. Most people walked or rode horseback. Then carriage makers began to use uniform parts to assemble their carriages. Often these parts were made by different manufacturers.

A hardware shop might make the nickel door handles and fine brass lamps. A coach company would make the upholstering, fringe, and tassels. Another company manufactured the springs; a second, the axle; a third, the locks for the doors. The carriage maker ordered the parts he needed and brought them to his shop, where he put the carriage together. Carriages were made faster and cheaper. Everyone wanted a carriage.

When horseless carriages (automobiles) were invented, a man named Henry Leland decided that automobiles could be made in parts as well as muskets. Leland had worked at the Springfield Armory and learned the Whitney system of uniform parts and machine tooling.

In 1906, Leland went to England and dismantled three Cadillacs. Just as Eli Whitney had demonstrated his muskets to the government officials, Leland put together the three cars, using their parts interchangeably. He proved that automobiles could be produced by the interchangeable parts system.

Henry Ford studied what Leland had done. Ford carried Eli
Whitney's system even further. He put out his small automobile
cheaply and quickly enough so that many people could own one.

Today it would be hard to look about and find an article that
was not influenced in its development by Whitney's ideas. In
the sky are airplanes. On the road are automobiles and bicycles.
In the home are television sets, washing machines, vacuum
cleaners, and electric trains.

MASS-PRODUCED GOODS THAT HAVE RESULTED FROM WHITNEY'S
SUCCESSFUL USE OF INTERCHANGEABLE PARTS

When something goes wrong with one of these products, repairs are convenient and less expensive than they would be if we could not buy new standard parts to replace the old ones. If the sewing machine breaks down, a part does not have to be specially made. Dealers keep uniform, interchangeable parts, made by the factory, to replace those that break down.

If an automobile tire blows out, the owner does not have to send his car back to the factory to have the tire replaced. He can go into any garage and buy a standard-size tire to fit the wheel on his car.

Even the manufacturers of such simple articles as light bulbs recognized the importance of the uniform, interchangeable parts system. They agreed on standard sizes. Thus a housewife may replace a burned-out bulb simply by screwing a new bulb into the socket.

All these men who learned and used and improved upon Eli Whitney's idea of interchangeable parts also thought much as Eli used to think. "What can I make that people need?" "How can I make it better and cheaper and faster, so that people can afford to buy it?"

When the men felt they had the answer, they worked hard, with faith in themselves and the thing they had decided to make, just as Eli Whitney did.

Chronology

1765   Born in Westborough, Mass.

1789   Entered Yale College, New Haven, Conn.

1792   Sailed to Savannah, Ga.

1793   Invented cotton gin.

1794   Whitney's cotton gin patented.

1798   Signed contract with the government to deliver ten thousand stand of arms.

1799   Built Mill Rock Arms Manufactory in New Haven, Conn.

1809   Delivered last shipment of stand of arms, fulfilling his contract of 1798 with the government.

1812   Signed second contract with the government to make fifteen thousand firearms.

1817   Married Henrietta Frances Edwards.

1818   Built plain milling machine.

1825   Died in New Haven, Conn.

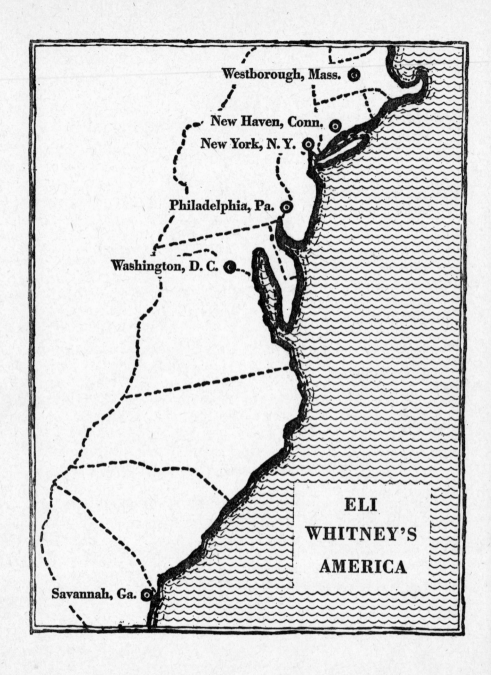

Westborough, Mass.

New Haven, Conn.

New York, N. Y.

Philadelphia, Pa.

Washington, D. C.

Savannah, Ga.

ELI
WHITNEY'S
AMERICA

Index

Mill Rock Arms Manufactory 55
Mill village 35
Miller 14–16, 19
Milling machine 38, 39, 55
Millsite 26
Muskets 4, 23 ff., 28 ff., 36, 49, 55;
    also see Stand of arms

Nails 4, 6

Patent 19, 21, 55
Plantation 15, 16, 21

Quill pen 9

Reaper 46
Revolutionary War 4, 6, 15, 25

Schoolhouse 9
Screw press 22
"Sea island cotton" 15
Sewing machines 45, 52
Short-staple cotton 16
Smeaton, John 12
South, the 15, 16, 19, 21
Stand of arms 24, 28, 36, 55; *also
    see* Muskets
Stebbins 16, 36, 37
Stepmother 3, 7

Teaching 7, 9, 14
Television sets 50
Terry 44
Thirteen Colonies 1, 23
Thomas, Seth 44

United States government: *see*
    Government

Vacuum cleaners 50

War of 1812 37
Washing machines 50
Watt's steam engine 12
Whitney, Ben 2
Whitney, Eli: born, 1, 55; builds
    gun factory, 26, 55; contract ful-
    filled, 36, 55; at college, 10–13;
    children, 41; demonstrates mus-
    kets, 30–32; died, 55; makes:
    hatpins, 6, knife, 3, milling ma-
    chine, 38, 55, nails, 4, screw
    press, 22; marries, 41, 55; at Mrs.
    Greene's, 15–19; nephews, 40; re-
    pairs instrument, 12; signs con-
    tract, 25, 55; teaching, 7, 9, 14
Whitney, Eli (father) 1, 2, 3
Whitney, Eli, Jr. (son) 41, 42
Whitney, Elizabeth 2, 4, 40
Whitney, Elizabeth (Fay) 1
Whitney farm 1, 2
Whitney, Josiah 2
Wilkinson, John 12
Winchester Arms 42
Wolcott, Secretary: argues for con-
    tract, 29; considers proposal, 24;
    invention for, 41; letter from, 22;
    letter to: 26, 28, 34; sees demon-
    stration, 30

Yale College 10, 40, 41, 55

58